SPACE TOURISM MARKET DEVELOPMENT STRATEGIES

EDITION 2

JOHN LOK

Copyright © John Lok
All Rights Reserved.

Contents

Preface

Introduction

This book divides two part. The first part explains how to predict future space tourism consumer behavior and the second part explains how to implement space organizational strategy.

This book first part researchs two questions: What factors will raise space tourism leisure desire to space travelling planners? How to solve any challenges to raise space travelling planner individual space travel leisure desire?

I shall apply psychology methods to attempt to predict space tourism planner individual space tourism desire in whole future space tourism leisure market development.

Whether will future space tourism market development be popular to be accepted one kind of travelling leisure to any travelling consumers in global? What factors can influence traveler prefer to choose space tourism entertainment more than general Earth tourism entertainment? How to influence future space tourism traveler individual space travel entertainment desire to be more stronger? How to attract travelers to feel space tourism entertainment which is one kind of real meaning of life travel leisure at least one time spending?

I write this book second part aims to give my opinions to let readers to feel how operate or manage one space exploration organization in success.I shall indicate these different factors which influence one successful space exploration successfully. Such as effective organization culture and communication factor, management team and strategy factor, space flight safe factor etc. It is suitable to any readers who pursue to know how manage or operate one space exploration organization in success.

In this book, I shall follow travel psychologists and space tourism entertainment businessmen support view points to give my opinions to attempt to answer above questions. My readers will learn how to apply new space travel strategic knowledge to solve and predict future space tourism leisure consumer behavior more accurately.

Prologue

Content of contents

(3) On space tourism leisure organization managment aspect

(5) On space objective aspect

Chapter Six

Space tourism and destinations market development p.87-100

Reference p.101

part two space tourism organizational strategy

Chapter Seven

Space flight safe factor p.102-108

Chapter Eignt

Space exploration organization mission and strategy p.109-119

- Space exploration
- organization communication strategy

Chapter Nine

Space exploration organization's human space life science factor

- What is human space life science strategy? p.120-140
  - How can human space life science strategy implement?
    - Situation analysis
    - What are space life science strategy goals?

Health innovation goal

- Prediction on future trends in human space flight and future space human life science strategy relationship.

● Why does Japan space organization consider space human life science?

Space tourism market development

Content of contents
part one Space tourism market development
Chapter One

● organization
communication strategy

Chapter Nine
Space exploration organization's
human space life science factor
● What is human space life
science strategy? p.120-140

● How can human space life science
● strategy implement?

● Situation analysis

● What are space life science
strategy goals?

Health innovation goal

● Prediction on future trends in
human space flight and future
space human life science strategy relationship.

● Why does Japan space
organization consider space
human life science?

CHAPTER ONE

FUTURE SPACE TOURISM PSYCHOLOGY PREDICTION STRATEGY

● Psychology and economic environment changing both factors influence whole space tourism market leisure desire

How can psychology method predict space tourism leisure desire? I believe that it has relationship between the space tourism planner and the economic environment as well as his/her psychology as below:

Firstly, on the economic environment influence hand, it includs these both economic situations, either in the good economic environment, many people can earn high income and employers can supply many job number to provide to many people to work, then it will influence the space travelling planner has more space travelling desire. Otherwise, or in the bad economic, less people can earn high income and employers can not supply many job number to provide to many people to work, it will influence the space travelling planner has less space travelling desire.

Secondly, on these both the space travelling planner individual psychology influence hand, the space travelling planner will have these both aspects of individual psychological influence, it includes these both either positive or negative psychological influence aspectsas below:

On the positive psychological influence aspect, if the space travelling planner has confidence to the space travelling leisure company can provide safe, comfortable, good quality of one space travelling trip arrangement, good taste food arrangement, reasonable space ticket price and every reasonable space trip for space hotel living arrangement and space garden and space farming land visiting journey arrangement, even, space swimming pool and space sport centre and space cinema leisure arrangement to let whom to stay on the planet at least one day trip, it means not one short time space trip, e.g. the spacecraft only flies about half hour or one half. It can not fly to the planet to arrive its space station destination to stay to let the space travelling planner to live at the space hotel at least one night. Then the space travelling planner will have more desire to choose to catch the space tourism leisure company's spacecraft to travel to space.

Otherwise, on the negative psychological influence aspect, if the space travelling planner lacks confidence to the space travelling leisure company can provide safe, comfortable, good quality of one space travelling trip arrangement, good taste food arrangement, reasonable space ticket price and every reasonable space trip for space hotel living arrangement and space garden and space farming land visiting journey arrangement, even, space swimming pool and space sport centre and space cinema leisure arrangement to let whom to stay on the planet at least one day trip, it means not one short time space trip, e.g. the spacecraft only flies about half hour or one half. It can not fly to the planet to arrive its space station destination to stay to let the space travelling planner to live at the space hotel at least one night. Then the space travelling planner will have less desire to choose to catch the space tourism leisure company's spacecraft to travel to space.

Hence, it seems economic environment changing factor and the space travelling planner's confidence factor to the space tourism leisure providers will influence the whole space travelling market whose space travelling consumer's space travelling leisure consumption desire to be more or less. So, any one space tourism provider can not neglect these both factors how to influence whose customer consumption desire.

● space tourism strategy

Future any space tourism leisure business needs have good business plan to outline the space tourism leisure business in these aspects , such as: different space tourism destinations of every space tourism journey, technical , financial and regulatory factors for growing space tourism leisure consumption into any one kind of unique artificial intelligent space tourism journey for identified passenger target group.

All how to design one space tourism business development plan to attempt to predict whether what trends will influence how every different kinds of identified space tourism journey in order to achieve passenger number growing aim as well as how to achieve one attractive space tourism leisure to satisfy future space tourism passenger individual space travel needs more easily.

I shall indicate what aspects to future every space tourism traveler who will consider in order to reduce the space tourism traveler personal worry to catch any pace boats to leave our Earth to fly to other planets to travel.

I recommend that any space tourism leisure organizations need to concern these aspects in their space tourism leisure business plan as below:

(1) safe space tourism journey

On first aspect concerns safe space tourism journey plan to let all space tourism travelers will considerate safe issue. They must ensure space boats that is safe to catch them to fly to planets in their space journeys. So, any space tourism leisure business will utilize previous flight rated and proven technologies to form the basis for manufacturing spacecraft vehicles, and will incorporate the latest modern avionics and flight systems for ensuring safety, reliability and economical operation in order to reduce any space tourism traveler personal worry to catch any spacecraft.

So, the space tourism safe journey plan is one very important factor to influence space tourism consumer number for them if any one of space tourism leisure business hoped they can grow the space tourism consumer number for long term. For example, the space boat flight hardware must often be maintained at the space station. It is needed to be considered by space boat experts as risky, extremely expensive and potentially sensitive. To aims to ensure spacecraft will offer an economical and safe alternative for any satellite manufacturers and other space tourism entertainment organizations have a desire or requirement for space tourism flight.

(2) reduction cost expense plan

On second aspect concerns reduction cost expense plan, any space tourism entertainment organizations need have the experience and capacity for safely launching a fully loaded , including space tourism passengers and passenger individual cargo for every spacecraft tourism journey. As a result of outsourcing the launch role to a major contractor, the space tourism pilot can concentrate on space boat crews flight training, planning space tourism passenger cargo capacity and preparing space flight manifests , and will as a result, avoid the expense of maintaining a launch operation on a daily basis.

In addition, by outsourcing the spacecraft manufacturing, it can avoid spending millions of dollar on facilities and equipment infrastructure and engineering manufacturing expertise.

(3) achieve any space tourism mission plan

On third aspect concerns how to achieve any space tourism mission. Every space tourism mission must be ensure that reliable service is provided to satisfy every space tourism passenger personal space traveler needs and let them to enjoy in their whole space tourism journey, let them to catch a big aircraft in comfortable environment of technologically sophisticated space boat, reasonable and competitive every time space tourism flight ticket price plan is developed and properly revised every time space tourism ticket price when performing their assigned every different space tourism journey mission.

Hence, the space tourism leisure company will provide one careful selected space tourism destination , e.g. Mar planet space tourism journey, Moon planet space tourism journey or no any space destination journey, it means that the space craft only needs to fly one circle around between Earth and Moon space journey etc. that are capable of meeting the requirements of travelling into Earth orbit. So, any space tourism journey must emphasize affordability, reliability, safety, customer service and responsiveness in responding to every client's space tourism journey requirements. Hence, any one of space tourism journey must have clear space journey mission and objective to satisfy any space traveler client target needs.

CHAPTER TWO

METHODS TO RAISE SPACE TRAVELER NUMBER

Future space tourism will be one kind of new travel leisure market for any new space travel leisure companies to enter this undiscovered market in the beginning. However, how to predict future 10 to 20 years , even more space traveler number that is one important issue to any new space tourism leisure companies.

I think that space tourism leisure companies need to define what kinds of space travel leisure service to be provided to space travelling passengers, however, what age group of space passengers who will be their space travelling target client. For example, their space travel leisure must provide any flight operation that takes one or more passengers beyond the altitude of 100 km and thus into space to let space travelling passengers who have fun, exciting space travelling feeling.

Anyway, for any kind of space tourism (leisure space travel) journey, space tourism leisure company needs anyone to be bring customer satisfaction, it is a plan or predictive methods to measure how to let every space travelling passenger to feel comfortable when they are catching the spacecraft (space flying product) and they can have enjoyable and fun or exciting feeling when they have need providing any space tourism journey, services meet or surpass customer expectations.

Thus, any space tourism leisure company needs to evaluate the degree of every time space tourism journey's customer satisfaction and customer satisfaction is also always evaluated in relationship to the every time ticket price of the space tourism journey. So, the space tourism leisure company will predict the next time of what the space tourism journey of passenger number is more accurate, after it has evaluated what degree of every time space tourism journey's customer satisfaction is. It aims to gather their opinions to find which aspects that they need to revise, e.g. choosing where will be the next time space tourism journey destination, how to improve spacecraft staff's service attitude and performance to serve to their space tourism passengers when they are catching the spacecraft, to evaluate whether the spacecraft can provide comfortable and safe environment to let them to catch in order to let the next time space travelling passengers can feel satisfactory and enjoyable when they are catching the space tourism leisure's spacecraft to fly to anywhere in space.

In general, the expectation of factors space passengers include the following customer value elements, such as below:

● viewing space and the Earth.

● experiencing weightlessness and being able to float freely in zero gravity.

● experiencing pre-flight astronaut training and related sensations.

● communicating from space to significant others.

● being able to discuss the adventure in an informed way.

● having astronaut like documentation and memorabilia.

These objectives need to be combined with, sometimes conflicting constraints, such as guaranteed safe return, limited training time, reasonable comfort, and minimum medical restrictions. All these above issues which will be every space travelling passenger considerate matters before they choose the space tourism leisure company to catch its spacecraft to fly to space. So, all these factors will influence the next time space passenger number. Any space tourism leisure company can not neglect how to solve these all matters before they decide when their next time space tourism journey to be achieved.

Consequently, if the space craft tourism leisure company could revise what aspects of its last space tourism journey to find what are its wrong or weakness or unattractive challenges to cause any one space travelling passenger who feels unsatisfactory. Then, it can have more effort to concentrate on improving its next space tourism journey to raise its space tourism service performance level , e.g. people, food, leisure etc. service aspects and its space tourism product quality level, e.g. proving comfortable spacecraft facilities to let space travelling passengers to catch in whole spacecraft tourism journey. Then, it will have more confidence to achieve the raising space travelling passenger number.

● What is the prediction space travelling passenger desire method ?

The prediction space travelling passenger individual desire method can be one survey investigation method. When every time spacecraft finishes space tourism journey mission, after all space tourism passengers catch the spacecraft to arrive earth from space. When they arrive earth space station destination, then the space tourism leisure company can arrange survey investigation staffs to enquire their feeling for this time space tourism journey immediately.

The survey content can include as below:

Do you feel satisfactory or unsatisfactory to which aspects of this time space tourism journey?

(1) On service aspect questions include as below:

(a) Do you feel space food taste is good?

(b) Do you enjoy this time space tourism journey arrangement?

(c) Do you feel satisfactory to space staff
service performance?

(d) If you have unsatisfactory feeling for any one of above questions, which aspect issue cause you feel unsatisfactory to explain to let us to know in order to us to revise our service performance.

(2) On product aspect questions include as below:

(a) Do you feel comfortable when you are catching our spacecraft in whole space tourism journey?

(b) If you feel comfortable , may you explain the reasons what aspects of our spacecraft has weakness to cause you feel uncomfortable?

(c) Do you feel safe when you are catching our spacecraft in whole space tourism journey?

(d) If you feel unsafe, may you explain the reasons what aspects of our spacecraft has weakness to cause you feel unsafe?

Finally, we thank your ideas to be given to let us know how to improve our every time future space tourism journey in order to find what challenge cause our service performance and product quality which can not satisfy your needs. So, we shall improve to avoid future challenges continue occur.

Our mission is achievement of 100% satisfactory level to our every space travelling passenger individual feeling. Also, we hope that you can choose our space tourism leisure service again, when you have another time space tourism leisure desire need. However, we shall revise to improve our service performance and product quality to be better, after collecting your ideas from this time survey investigation. I think you spend time to give your ideas from this survey investigation faithfully.

So, survey investigation method will be one important idea gathering tool to help any space tourism leisure company to revise the weaknesses to raise or improve future every time space tourism journey service performance and product quality to achieve raising competitive effort in this new space tourism leisure market.

Hence, survey investigation method will be the best idea gathering method to predict how space travelling passenger emotion or desire need will change in order to achieve the objective of raising every time space tourism journey future space travelling passenger number more easily for every space tourism leisure company.

● The prediction of price factor influences space traveler number

The space tourism leisure organizations indicate the total cost of a trip into space is rapidly coming down from the initial price level of about US$600,000, it is obvious that the space travelling customer base is going to be rather small. Typical customers tend to belong to the top 1% income bracket. They also indicate that the price comes down , it is expected that new space travelling customer groups will enter the space tourism leisure market.

Typical new customers include people in other brackets with one-of-a kind incomes, such as inheritance or business sold. There are indications that those types of customers are becoming interested in spending on an once-in-a lifetime space experience. Therefore, the growth of the space tourism market is highly sensitive to customer satisfaction and how it is communicated through various media.

This will establish the status factors of space tourism and corresponding brand reputation service providers. They also suggest that any operator monitors space travelling customer satisfaction closely, as it will help developing increasingly accurate estimates of how the space tourism leisure market will develop.

Hence, it seems that every time space tourism journey price variable factor will influence the time space tourism of customer individual leisure desire and the space tourism passenger number. For example, the minimum price goal foe a variable space tourism business is currently estimate to be below US$3000-4000/kg for a round -trip depending on variable configuration and operation size. At this price, they estimate that somewhat over 1 % of the high income earners are potential customers.

However, for significant volume growth the longer term

goal should be below US$2000/kg for a typical passenger, baggage and supplies. The lower price will probably open space tourism to a broader population, expanding the customer base and altering expectations. beyond this point space tourism will become into a travelling competitive leisure commodity, price competition will ensure and service providers need to rethink their space tourism marketing and branding and price strategies.

I shall also recommend how to attract the potential customers successfully. First, space operators need to pay special attention to the right level of customer services. Second, various preparatory customer operations cost, such as a travel to the launch site, space tourism destination accommodation, pre-flight training, medical check-ups and equipment my add up to between 10 to 15 % of the actual space travel cost. Thurs, solving the right balance between services offered and cost of client operation in order to earn the largest intangible benefits, such as loyalty, confidence, leisure enjoyment, comfortable space travelling journey as well as tangible benefits, such as profit, spacecraft manufacturing facilities, space stations, space hotels , space swimming pools, space gardens, space cinema etc. which are built to similar to earth building facilities to satisfy space travelers' needs.

CHAPTER THREE

THE INFLUENTIAL FACTORS PERSUADE TRAVELERS CHOOSE SPACE TOURISM

Nowadays, our earth is no longer an adventurous enough place for some experienced tourists. Space tourism will be a new sector of adventure tourism, which is in the near future will be fast becoming a new tourism leisure opportunity for experiencing the unknown. Of one day, space tourism is able to reach the mass tourism phase, due to improved safety and decreased operation costs, a future space tourist will possibly only need minimal training to cope with the zero cost.

Space tourism is quite well established with visits to space attraction and launch sites, and it is a wealthy trips to the international space station for any space tourism travelers. However, if any space tourism leisure companies can attempt to find what the most influential factors are to persuade travelers feel attraction more than travelling in our earth.

It aims to let travelers to choose space travelling more than earth travelling when they feel travelling leisure need. I shall indicate what will be the most important influential factors to persuade travelers to choose space tourism more than earth tourism as below:

Firstly, I shall argue that the majority of different new space tourism journey destinations will be needed to find to satisfy different aged space travelers and different income space tourism consumers' needs. For example, the rich people have effort to consume longer time and reach any space tourism destinations where are far away from our earth of their every space tourism journey.

Otherwise, the middle income people will choose shorter space tourism journey distance from our earth and short time space tourism journey. Also, younger space tourism clients can accept more longer journey time, exciting fast speed spacecraft flying journey. Otherwise, old space tourism clients can only accept comfortable and shorter time safe space journey. So, it seems that safety, comfortable feeling, shorter time space tourism journey won't be one important influential factor to excite any young people who choose to consume space tourism leisure. Otherwise, safety, comfortable feeling, shorter time space tourism journey will be one important influential factor to excite any old people who choose to consume space tourism leisure.

Secondly, the another most important influential factor to excite space travelers to choose space tourism , it concerns whether the space travelers will feel what tourists benefits can be earned from a substantial variety of destinations choice. In general, space tourism with those of aviation, space travelers will hope space tourism will be travelling distances by air in a very short time, safely and comfortably, to bring them to arrive any space planet destinations when spacecraft reaches any space stations to stay in any space destinations.

Hence, space destination factor will bring important influential choice to any space destination journeys. As a result of the space technological tourism boom, the number of potential different space destination, choice attractions have grown with far fewer places on earth to which human do have access yet. However, the ultimate different space destinations to which many of us dream is not on earth, but as least 100 km above us, anywhere in space any planets.

If the space tourism leisure company can provide different space tourism destination choices to young or old age both space traveler target consumer groups. They will feel a real holiday when they will be able to enjoy a great image of the earth from planets. It might mean that every space tourism journey can provide different space tourism destination to let space travelers have another new travelling destinations where are far from our earth anywhere.

Hence, the different space tourism destinations will give them an unforgettable advventure. Think of how it would be to be able to check in at a " billion strategy" luxury hotel in space one planet, it means that the space planet destination can provide one luxury hotel to let space travelers to live one night or more in the space planet destination, how it would be to schedule the space traveler' vacation at one of the space tourism leisure company luxury resorts on the Moon or Mars.

This images seem from science fiction movies, but one should not forget that 100 years ago, the Wright brothers, aviation pioneers inventors and builders of the air plane, would not have imagined how, every day it is possible that future spacecraft can fly to any planets to let human have chance to stay in the space hotel one night or more.

Consequently, space destination choice and space tourism journey service performance, aviation safety, ticket price and leisure satisfactory feeling which will be important influential factors to attract future space travelers to choose space tourism leisure to replace earth tourism leisure in future one day.

CHAPTER FOUR

Raising Space Tourism Leisure Consumption Strategies

Although, space tourism industry is a real enjoyment and exciting travelling leisure to human. It is possible that human will choose to consume space tourism leisure to replace earth tourism leisure, if human felt that earth tourism leisure is not attractive to them to consume to go to anywhere to travel in their leisure time.

But, I believe that space tourism industry has still many factors to influence human to choose to consume space tourism leisure, even they will consider space tourism leisure consumption I is only one time space tourism in their life time. Hence, space tourism companies ought achieve this aim to persuade or attract everyone prefer to spend space tourism leisure at least one time in their life, then it can represent success. However, I think to achieve this aim, it has these challenges to influence their success, even they believe space tourism leisure business is one potential attractive travel entertainment business. These challenges include such as: expensive space tourism ticket price issue, catching spacecraft safe issue, space traveler personal body health issue, age issue, family and friend relationship influence issue, working time and holiday time arrangement issue, the space trip arrangement issue, weather issue etc. different challenges, which will have possible to influence every space tourism planner either who decide change to cancel the time space tourism plan, or forgive to choose space tourism leisure in their life forever.

Hence, how to raise space tourism leisure consumption desire will be one considerable matter for any space tourism leisure businessmen. I shall indicate my personal three aspect of strategical opinions to let them to know how to raise every space tourism planner individual space tourism leisure consumption desire to avoid every time space tourism passenger number will have decrease failure chance as below:

● (1) Strategic opinion

On the first aspect of strategic opinion, I feel that the space education tutor can teach new space knowledge to let every space traveler to learn any new space and earth knowledge during he/she is catching on the spacecraft in personal contact learning experience environment which can raise space tourism consumption desire. The reason is because the space tourism leisure traveler can raise extra space and earth learning knowledge when they can catch the spacecraft to fly and contact the space environment to learn and feel what the differences are between space and earth by himself or herself. Hence, it is very attractive to the space traveler student target group and I believe that their parents will encourage their sons or daughters to participate the time of space trip and they are more preferable to help them to buy the time space trip ticket, due to their sons and daughters can learn any space knowledge when they are studying. Moreover, every space traveler will feel surprise to learn any new space and earth knowledge from the space tutor's teaching, due to he/she is unknown that this space travel trip includes learning space and earth knowledge.

I suggest that the space tourism leisure businessmen can give learning opportunity to every travel trip space travelers to feel that this space actual environment can bring what disadvantages or advantages to influence our earth when they are catching aircraft to fly to space to travel in every space trip. The space and earth learning knowledge can include these two aspects of space learning knowledge and experience below:

On the teaching of space environment learning knowledge hand, the topics can include as below:

Firstly the space learning topic can concern how space environment influences water and hydrated minerals change , they can learn what our drinking water function how is applied to space environment. For example, in the space environment, they can learn and attempt to feel that how water can be used in protecting astronauts against harmful radiation from the sun and cosmic rays by cloaking spacecraft with a thin layer of water in the actual space environment as well as the space travelers can also feel water is same as fuel when they are catching the spacecraft, they can feel the water is heavy to transport into space when they are catching the spacecraft to fly to space during their whole space tourism journey.

Moreover, when their spacecraft reaches anyone of planets and it stays on the planet's space station, e.g. Moon space station. They can learn how to attempt to contact the hydrated minerals to learn and feel what they contained in some asteroids may be possible sources of water and fuel in the actual space environment. When they are walking in actual space environment, such as Moon planet, they can contact or touch this hydrated minerals to learn how water molecules can be extracted and separated chemically to produce hydrogen fuel knowledge in the actual space environment. This is one exciting space learning experience to the space travelling student passengers.

Secondly the space learning topic can concern how human fights space threats , even when their whole space leisure journey, the space science teacher can let the space trip student passengers to feel that they are learning new space knowledge between the space science teacher and whose space trip student passengers. Such as how to protect our earth knowledge: Teaching them to know when will be threats to our earth from space. The space science teacher can explain how this space threating environment influences our life safety and let them to feel that a mass extinction can be triggered if an asteroid 10 kilometers across hit the earth. Even being the apex species in the food chain did not space carnivorous dinosaurs from such disaster, who knows if this terrifying scene won't happen before our eyes? So, the space travelers can image and feel how the space threating environment can influence their life safety in the actual space environment as well as the space science teacher can let whose space travelers to feel and image the actual earth disaster will possible happen suddenly to let they feel afraid in the actual space environment. Also the space science teacher can teach how our earth can fright the space stones attack to let the space traveler to know, when an impactor targets an asteroid for a controlled well-times wallop. The collision will change the asteroid's momentum, deflecting it from its original orbital path which intersects with that of the earth. So, at the moment, the space travelers can image they are a larger spacecraft near an asteroid which can also change the path. Given enough time, the gravitational pull from the spacecraft will be able to steer the asteroid away from the earth. So, every space traveler will feel that they are catching the spacecraft in the safe space environment to avoid the Earth disaster from space sudden unpredictable attack.

It is more fun real space tourism knowledge learning feel to let every space traveler has chance to learn any new space science knowledge when he/she is catching the spacecraft to fly to space to travel. Hence, one successful space trip ought include trip and learning experience both contents in order to raise every the space tourism planner individual space trip consumption desire.

● (2) Strategic opinion

On the second aspect of strategic opinion, space tourism leisure companies need to let planning travelers feel that anyone of space tourism leisure is very different to general tourism leisure. In general, tourism leisure is visiting at least one night for leisure and holiday, business or other tourism purposes in Earth only. Otherwise, space tourism leisure is other kind of an unique trip leisure or entertainment method, e.g. the space traveler can catch the spacecraft to visit any planets to stay to live at the planet's space hotel at least one night, e.g. Future potential populated Moon or Mars space hotel space trip. Moreover, the space travel companies ought give chance to let them to feel what weightless feeling is in weightlessness environment when they are walking on Moon or other planets in possible. Even, they can attempt to build these entertainment facilities, instead of space hotels, such as space swimming pools, space gardens, space cinema etc. building facilities. It aims to let them to feel what the differences between Earth and space life when they are walking on the Moon, when they are swimming on the space pools, when they are living in space hotels, when they are watching movies in space cinemas, when they are seeing flowers and different species of planets and fruits. e.g. oranges, apples, bananas, and vegetable and potatoes and tomatoes in space gardens. It is very exciting and fun space trip life experience between one days to seven days. So, they believe that they must not feel these space life experience if they do not choose to participate this time space trip planning journey by the space trip company preparation.

Also, due to that the space tourism passengers need to the pre-flight checks and training before they ensure to qualify to permit to participate the space trip. So space travel companies need to concern how to take care their health check and training matter considerately. It aims to let every space traveler will feel a market segment with fitness and extreme experiences as well as he/she will become popular with a market segment passenger to the space tourism leisure company, although he/she must not guarantee to pass the space training and/or pre-flight health checks to permit to participate the space trip. However, he/she can believe that he/she is one worth space travelling passenger to the space tourism leisure company, even this time pre-flight health check or/and the short time space trip training requirements are failure. However, the space tourism leisure company must need to let all pre-flight health check and space trip training passengers to feel that it is only one space tourism which can give them and let customers view the space travel is as the ultimate showcase for health, even though a majority of the population can pass the pre-flight medical and other tests in order to raise their confidence and safety to catch the spacecraft to fly to space to travel when they are confirmed to pass these tests to permit to catch the spacecraft later.

In general, the expectations of future space passengers include the following customer value elements, such as below:

● Viewing space and the Earth.

● Experiencing weightlessness and experiencing pre-flight astronaut training and related sensations.

● Communicating from space to significant others.

● Being able to discuss the adventure in an informed way.

● Having astronaut-like documentation and memorabilia.

● Enjoying one exciting and fun space trip.

However, instead of considering these objectives need to be combined with, sometimes conflicting , constraints such as guaranteed safe, return , limited training time, reasonable comfort, and minimum medical restrictions. So, space tourism companies need to reduce every space traveler individual worries before they decide to make the time of space tourism journey. Then, it can increase their confidence to raise their space tourism consumption desire more successfully.

Consequently, instead of these consideration, a space travel operator must pay attention to the total customer experience over the entire customer process, starting from how the service is presented, proposed and sold. The service package must include training, instructions, travel to the launch site and various post. Travel activities to generate maximum customer satisfaction and brand building opportunity.

● (3) Strategic opinion

On the final aspect of strategic opinion, I think any space tourism companies space tourism companies need to consider every time space tourism ticket price and space tourism trip issues. It is important factor to influence every space traveler individual consumption desire. Due to space trip ticket price must be more expensive to compare common Earth trip travelling ticket price, so this kind of tourism leisure market target customer will be the rich and high income customer group.

On the space trip ticket challenge issue, despite that fact the total cost of a trip into space is rapidly coming down from the initial price level of about US$60,000, it is obvious that the customer base is going to be rather small and the client target customer is only high income or rich consumer group. Typical customers tend to belong to the top of the top 1% income bracket. So, ensures that space traveler number must be less than common Earth traveler number. Also, such as the space trip ticket price, it is expected that new middle rich level or middle high level income customer target group will enter the space trip leisure market, when every space trip ticket price falls down about 1% Typical new customers include people in other income brackets with one-of-a-kind incomes, such as inheritance or business sold space traveler target group. These people will be space travel new client group, when its every space trip ticket price can be reduced to close 1 to 2 % nearly. If any space tourism leisure companies expect to attract new rich and/or high income target customer group to choose any one kind of space trip journey planning to consume.

These are indications that these types of customers are becoming interested in spending on an once-in-a-lifetime space experience. Therefore, the growth of the space tourism market is highly sensitive to customer satisfaction and how it is communicated through the various media. This will establish the status –factor of space tourism, and corresponding brand reputation of service providers. The minimum price goal for a variable space tourism business is currently estimate to be below US$3-4000/kg for a round-trip depending on vehicle configuration. So, space travel leisure companies need to concern every round space trip cost, it can depend on the space vehicle number and weight issue to influence every space trip ticket price variable to achieve how much it can earn.

On space journey design factor aspect, it includes these different facilities aspects how to design, because future space travelling consumers will concern whether the space travel company can provide special entertainment to satisfy their needs. The facilities include as below:

How to design space hotels to let them to live in comfortable space environment and eat the best taste and fresh food quality when the cookers need to cook in the space hotel in the space environment? How to design space swimming pools to let them to swim in safe space environment? How to design space sport centers to let them to run more easily in one space sport warm and safe environment? How to design one space garden to let them to see different species of Earth flowers, or plants? How to design one space farming land to let them to see different species of Earth fruits, vegetables, tomatoes, potatoes etc.

fresh foods growth in warm and safe space farming land environment? How to design one space cinema to let them to watch movies in one safe and warm space cinema environment? All these facilities will be any one of future space trip's' important and attractive space trip leisure facilities to influence every space traveler to choose to buy the space tourism leisure company's space trip leisure service.

Instead of these space building entertainment facilities, they also need to concern how the space vehicle entertainment tools are provided the entertainment service to satisfy their needs. When the space travelers can sit on the space vehicles to move on any planets' lands, such as Moon. A number of space vehicle options exist in the market, mainly differing based on the seat capacity as well as the in-flight experience level offered. The typical space vehicle solution is a small, relatively light weight spacecraft taking between 2 to 10 passengers. The number of passengers depends on the service level, amenities and extra offered. The trip typically lasts about 10 hours and of which about 4 hours are spent in space. The main attraction is the weightless time after in space. The main attraction is the weightless time after re-entry has started. It is a rather low-G technology and therefore the medical requirements for participants are nor very high.

Consequently, the space vehicles, space leisure building facilities, the space trip reasonable price ticket level, every safe space trip journey arrangement, clean and fresh and good taste space food arrangement, space traveler individual real learning experience etc. these factors will be the main influential factors to raise the space tourism leisure company's competitive effort and the space traveler consumer individual consumption desire to the space tourism leisure company in the future.

CHAPTER FIVE

SPACE TRAVEL MARKETING STRATEGY

Any space travel organization needs have good marketing strategy to prepare how to operate its space travelling leisure business in order to attract many space travelling clients to choose its space travelling service. I shall indicate these different strategies aspects whey they are needed to be concerned as below:

(1) On concept of spacecraft design aspect

Firstly, on concept aspect, any one space travelling leisure company needs have at least one spacecraft to catch clients to fly to space to travel. So how to design the spacecraft and its quality and safety and comfortable environment spacecraft machine concept aspect issue which is one challenge to be concerned. Because many space travelling passengers ususally concern whether the spacecraft is safe, comfortable , good quality, as well as the space travelling leisure providers also need to concern whether the spacecraft is less time and energy saving efficient use, less manufactory operating cost and durable. In general, space travelling leisure provider expects the spacecraft or spacecraft vehicle can be uesed long time. The spacecraft will be expected to utilize previous flight rated and proven technologies to from the basis for manufacturing spacecraft vehicles , and will incorporate the latest modern avionics and flight system for answering safety, reliability and economical operation.

In general, the spacecraft will be designed to carry two crew and approximately, 10,000 pounds of cargo, depending on the ultimate weight of the spacecraft. Relying on flight hardware to maintain the space station, such as Moon or Mar space station is fpr any space travelling spacecrafts to reach these space travelling destinations to stay, it is also need to consider by many space travelling experts as risky, extremely, expensive cost sensitive for any space station travelling destination design arrangement in order to future every spacecraft can fly to any planets to stay on its space station safely.

● Outsourcing spacecraft concept design strategy

As a result, outsourcing strategy is one good method to help them to reduce cost in order to achieve to let every space travel passenger has safe space journey experience and capacity for safely launching a fully loaded (including crew and cargo). Outsourcing strategy is the launch role to a major contracor, they can concentrate on crew flight training, planning all passnegers and cargo capacoty, and preparing flight manifests, and will as a result, avoid the expense of maintaining a launch operation on a daily basis. In addition, by outsoucing the spacecraft manufacturing, the space travelling provider can avoid spending millions of dollars on facilities and equipment infrastructure and engineering manufacturing expertise.

(2) On deciding misson aspect

Secondly, on mission aspect, any space travelling journey needs have a clear mission to be planned how to achieve in order to ensure every space travelling passenger feel satisfactory in the space travelling journey. So, every whole space travelling journey arrangement, e.g. where will be the space travelling destination, how to check every space travelling planned passengers' bodies whether who are health to catch spacecraft to fly to space to travel or how to train every space travelling planned passenger to ensure whom can permit to catch spacecraft to fly to space to travel, how to arrange every space travelling journey entertainment and facilities to let either young or old age target passenger to enjoy the space trip to feel satisfactory, how to arrange different days of every space trip.

In the last few years, Virgin Galactic has been making new's headlines with its promises to provide space travel services, and announcement that it will soom offer, at quite a hefty price, trips to sub-orbit. It is generally agreed that sub-orbit exists 100 kilometres above the earth's sea-level (Von Der Dunk, 2012). Hence, Virgin Galactic will provide travel to where customers may experience weightlessness, as well as the sight of earth's curvature. Even more interesting is that Virgin Galactic is not the only company with such a mission,there are a few more that wish to offer the same type of service. For example, some companies even aim to provide an orbital type of flight.

Orbit flight suggests that humans would venture into outer space, where they might either orbit the earth or board the international space station (hereinafter: ISS). In addition, some envision space hotels, moon visitations and mining asteroids. Although at first such statement might seem for one must point out that a "space hotel" is already in earth's orbit and that diligent progress through flight tests is almost made the commercial aspect of regular space travel a reality; it is only the question of time and readiness for the companies to make their long-awaited and open a new industry of present day economics (Klemm & Markkanen, 2011; Berry , 2012).

So, every space travelling mission is to ensure that reliable, technologically-sophisicated competitively-priced flight certified spacecraft are designed and properly maintained when performing their every assigned space travelling journey mission. The space traveller leisure provider will need to provide a carefully selected array of techologies that are capable of meeting the requirements of travelling into earth orbit. It will emphasize affordability, reliability, safety, customer service and responsiveness in responding to customer's space travelling requirements.

For this space tourism leisure mission example, it many include these objectives , such as below:

One trip into space, sending a space vehicle of a certain make and with a specify capacity on a space mission, provides the various grades of a core service, such as a space mission including issues such as waiting and delivery times, personal attention and advice, amenities and facilities, ensure quality assurance, it is the planned and system activities implemented in a quality system. So that quality requirements for a product or service will be fulfilled. It aims at preventing high-risk adverse events, or reducing thei impact, provides excellent customer satisfaction, it is a measure of how products and services meet the space travelling customer expectations, customer satisfaction is also always evaluated in relationship of every space travelling ticket price of the space travelling entertainment service and spacecraft product comfortable environment feeling and good leisure arrangement for every space travelling leisure journey.

(3) On space tourism leisure organization managment aspect

Thirdly, on space tourism leisure organization management aspect, it is also important to influence efficient and excellent space service performance to be provided to satisfy every space travel organization management team needs to be consists of experienced professionals who have successfully management and operated companies specializing in the aerospace industry for a number of years.

Their knowledge and contacts within the space industry will prove invaluable in assisting the space tourism leisure provider in the achievement of its goals and objectives. In individuals on the team components that up a spacecraft tourism development organization, and have unique experience in the design, construction, operations and maintenance of the major functions will developing spacecraft for launching into orbit. Every spacecraft will be built and maintained utilizing the same high standards of quality, within budget and well within time constraints.

Hence, every space tourism provider needs have one excellent management leaders to manage every space tourism service staffs to serve passengers in order to achieve excellent service performance to let them every one to feel satisfactory, during their every space tourism journey (trip).

(4) On target audience prediction aspect

On target audience prediction aspect, every space trip needs have identifies target travelling passenger in order to concentrate to choose the most popular and satisfactory space travelling journey for their identified needs.

For primary audiences example, it can include space enthusiasts and educational families both. Space enthusiasts target are usually young people and they are only 20% over 65 age old people target space ethusiasts who will be the future potential space tourism target consumers as well as the educational families target who will aspect owning educational experience for children , who is the explicit reason to visit space, either he/she has interest in history of space exploration or he/she has interest in future of space exploration or he/she feels that spce trip looked like fun.

KSCVC Visots (2013) indicated that future top markets, ranked by high visitation against space enthusiasts and educational families space tourism passengers, the US cities will include: Orlando, NYC, Miami, Tampa Bay, Chicago, West plam, Philadelphia, Atlanta, Boston, Washington, DC and San Francisco cities. So, future US space travelling market will be the top one in the world.

(5) On space objective aspect

On space objective aspect, instead of any one space tourism leisure organization concerns how to achieve its mission to satisfy all space tourism passengers leisure needs. Although, it is the major missin for space tourism leisure industry. But they can not neglect what the objectives are in order to develop or achieve long term space tourism leisure missions more easily.

The objectives main open space key issues can include such

as: Providing an adequate supply of land to meet the future needs of strategic opn space links, natural areas and recreational facilities on any future space tourism destinations, increasing pressure for public access to open space areas with conservation values, competing interests between adjoining land use and development on public open space and its user groups, use of public open space and recreational resources for drainage purposes, raising higher space traveller hotel residential development placing increased pressure on the demand for public open space planet land use aim and developing public open space mor intensive leisure and sport activities on any future new space tourism planet destinations.

When the space tourism leisure providers have long term objectives to attempt to solve above these any one of key issues. It will ahve a more clear objective to achieve its long term space tourism leisure business market. It's long term objectives can include such as below:

To identify existing and future active and passive recreation needs and social trends of future space tourism visitors; to provide a wide range of high quality and accessible public open space public land areas to encourage physical activity and social interaction to meet the existing and future needs of space travelling visitors; to identify existing gaps in the public open space network and develop any different kinds of space trip arrangement to satisfy the different identified target space traveller individual needs; to protect enhance and increase landcrapt values of public open space land use; to recognize the hierarchy lof public open space assets; equitably distributing open space resources; access to facilities and a diverse range of opportunities to incorporate the drainage function in public open space travelling destination areas without detriment to safely, environmental, visual and recreational values.

So, these development of any space planets howo to use their lands objectives will bring long term space travelling destination beneficial advantages to raise to build the space hotels, space swimming pools, space gardens, space cinemas, space sport places to let future space travelers can stay in Mars or Moon planet destinations to enjoy these leisure facilities and they can feel which are similar to our earth leisure facilities attractively.

These space buildings are important to attract future space travellers to catch spacecraft to fly to Mars or Moon planet to travel in possible because it is fun and exciting space trip when these leisure facilities can be built on Moon or Mars to let space travellers to stay short days in either these two planets to live their space hotels. So how to build any one of these space leisure building which is another important objective for any future space tourism leisure business, instead of how to arrange any space destination trip objective. So, any space tourism leisure provider ought not neglect how to achieve these two main space tourism objectives.

However, these are key questions continually asked regarding the viability of space tourism. They concern financial, marketing and political communities. Their concerns can be best addredded in a properly, comprehensive business plan. Some questions can not be answered definitively at this time. However, knowledge of the concerns and developing space businesses in any space traveling leisure planning stages and efforts to raise capital in the following questions, every spce tourism leisure business leader needs to concern this questions as below:

Can the space tourism industry into a profitable enonomic industry?

Are challenges related to financing, marketing, business methodologies or a combination of all of these facets?

Can the proponents of space tourism to be proven business tools and methodologies in their presentation of an acceptable business plan?

Can at least a cost effective, certified passenger space tourism journey to be developed for space tourism?

What effects will influence space-tourism businesses of NASA begins selling seats on the US space shuttle to civilian space tourists?

All above questions will be every new space tourism leisure businessman who needs to concern questions in order to achieve whose marketing strategy more successfully. Consequently, marketing strategy is important to be prepared in order to follow corrective steps to achieve every space tourism leisure business missions and objectives more easily.

CHAPTER SIX

SPACE TOURISM AND DESTINATIONS MARKET DEVELOPMENT

Future space tourism entertainment business success. The space tourism service provider needs to concern whom the customers are. The group of respondents interested in and willing to pay for space tourism customers who will have these needs to satisfy their space tourism entertainment in their space tourism journey as below:

They need to feel there is no place like home, of all the attractive features with a flight into space, viewing the Earth from space rated highest, space tourism customers want to have fun, when asked about their spending. They can accept to spend the largest amount of income on travelling and vacation. So, these earth travelling customers can accept to spend experience space travlling journeys to enjoy their holidays needs.

However, if the space tourism company can provide lower prices. Then, it will attract many space tourism customers to choose it's space travelling entertainment service. So, its demand will increase. In fact, orbital space travel is a fairly elastic market, there are significant jumps in demand when the service price drops to US $10 million and again at US$1 million. They must not accept physical discomfort post-space tourism flight. So , if the space tourism service provider can not provide physical comfort post-flight to its customers, then this poor space tourism service will influence its further space tourism customers number to be reduced.

However , one US space travel entertainment report indicated the demand for public space travel entertainment service prediction. A presentation of forecaste indicated that space travel projects , due to 2021 year, over 15,000 passengers could be flying annually, presenting revenues in excess of US$700 million. By 2021 year, the report also forecasted 60 passengers may be flying annually, representing revenues in excess of US$300 million.

The most important thing about on-orbit destination is options. The space travelling organizational report also estimated that an increase in demand would result from having commercial on-orbit facility available, predicting a total of 533 passengers over the forecast period, a 32 percent increae over the baseline forecast as the sole on-orbit destination option.

Despite above factors, a number of factors have effort to influence the future development of the market for public space travel. How to quantify and forecast the future demand for space tourism service more accurate. However, the space travelling organization report also indicated these factors can influence space tourism customers number, such as space transportation provison, space station design, space hotels facilities, space tourism life and accident insurance arrangement, space tourism destination journey and enentertainment arrangement, spae bank card service arrangement. This report aims to let every space tourism service provider has accurate insight to predict what future space tourism customer individual demand is in order to persuade every one to choose their every one different unique kind of space tourism entertainment activities attractively.

Is future public space tourism one popular spacecraft entertainment activity? It will demand on different factors to be accepted for different countries' public space tourism service provision. However, these are some countries begin to research public space tourism in order to let future space tourism passengers have one more public space tourism option , instead of private space tourim option.

Nowadays, government public spacecraft programs , these countries had been implementing. They include: Shenchou (China), NASV's and generation reusable lunch vehicle program (U.S.) as well as commercial spacecraft firms include: IC (Kistler Aerospace), SA (Space access), Statbooster (Starcraft boosters Inc.), Neptune (Interorbital systems). However, space tourism transportation will have one challenge to future space travellers, when there are currently no vehicles that can serve the suborbital space tourism market, a number of vehicles are under development. For example, the first team to privately build and fly a spacecraft capable of carrying. These people to 100 kilometers alitude twice in a two week period. Future space traveller service providers need to concern these questions: What is the size of its space tourism market? What is the growrh potential of the space tourism market? and What are the country's space tourism customer characteristcs for this country itself?

The space tourism service providers need to understand what Space tourism consumer individual space tourism entertainment need is, because every country's space tourism customers, they will have different space tourism unique needs and space tourism enterainment unique characteristics. Hence, the country's space tourism entertainment service providers need to familize what kinds of space tourism entertainment needs for themelves in order to atteact their choices more easily.

However private space tourism entertainment service providers need to concern when the public or government space tourism entertainment service providers will entert this space tourism entetainment market, instead of private space tourism enterainment service providers both competitors. Because it is possible that public space tourism entertainment service providers will provide similar or better or same space tourism entertainment service or arrangement similar or better or same space tourism journey arrangement or space tourism entertainment facilities. Then, the public space toursim entertainment service providers will influence their space tourism entertainment consumers number reduce when the private space tourism entertainment service consumers feel the public space tourism service providers can provide better space tourism service to compare them.

In conclusion, the consideration to the private space tourism service providers' issues who need to concern , they include how to design different kinds of space tourism entertainment facilities to let them to entertain as well as how to arrange attractive space tourim journeys to let them to enjoy their any space tourism journeys. Then, these two issues will be private space tourism entertainment service providers need to arrange how to achieve their space tourism stragegy attractively in order to win more space tourism choices in themselves country.

Reference

Klemm, G., & Markkanen, S. (2011). IN A Papathanassis (ed.) The long Tai , tourism (pp.95-103). Weisbaden, Germany : Gabler Verlag; Springer Fachmedien Weiesbaden GmbH.

KSCVC Visitors, 2013; MRI 2013 Market by Market

Von Der Dunk , F. (2012). The integrated approach. Regulating private human spaceflight as space activity, aircraft operation, and high-risk adventure tourism. Acta Astronautica, 92(2), 199-208.

space organizational strategy

CHAPTER SEVEN

SPACE FLIGHT SAFE FACTOR

To operate one space flight exploration organization, it needs to concern human safe flight factor. I shall indicate it needs to have these three stages to further develop its space exploration to continue to improve its safe space flight for every time of space flight.

Human future space flight missions will include these three stages to continue journey into space. The first stage is short term, NASA's return to flight after the Columbia accident. The second stage is mid term. What is needed to continue flying the shuttle fleet until a replacement means for human access to space and for other shuttle capabilities is available, and the third stage is long term, future directions for the kinds in space. Therefore, the space exploration organization can arrange the three stages to carry out any future space exploration activities. I believe it can improve every time of space flight more safe because it can ensure its space rocket engineering can be improved to raise safe level to let space people to catch to leave our Earth.

However, any human future space flight, which must be enhanced safety of flight when carry on any experimenting space flight exploration missions. Because NASA's safety performance is a very important factor to influence any space people confidence to catch every sky rocket to leave our Earth to do any space exploration activities. So, eliminating and catching rocket risks will be any beginning and end than during the middle of any space flight exploration journeys.

Space people's life is the most important assets of any space exploration journeys. Because of the dangers of ascent and re-entry, because of unknown space environment and because we are still relative new comers, operation of shuttle and indeed all human space flight must be viewed as a development activity.

Thus, any every time space flight exploration missions will need to encourage to invent new space transportation engines (machine) or fuel, e.g. nuclear fuel to reduce the any space exploration journey accident risks and achieves to spend the fastest time to arrive any new space exploration destination. Thus, I believe any new space exploration flight will improve the space transportation technology and invent more new fuel and new space rocket manufacturing materials for future human any unknown space exploration flight demand. The three stages of improving space transportation include as below:

The beginning stage, for example, the space shuttle is as somehow comparable to civil or military air transport. They are not comparable; the inherent risks of spaceflight are serious higher. The recognition of human spaceflight as a developmental activity requires a shift in focus from operations and meeting schedules to a concern for the risks involves. Thus, the space transportation tools will be improved to protect space passengers safety: the improving the ability to tolerate it, repairing the damage on a timely basis, reducing unforeseen events from the loss of crew and vehicle, exploring all options for survival, such as provisions for crew escape systems and safe havens , barring unwarranted departures from design standards and adjusting standards only under the most safety-driven process.

The mid-term stage, the present shuttle is not very safe to fly in space. Thus, focus on safe return to flight is very important to every space flight journey rules , they leave Earth and arrive any another new planet destination, then come back our Earth again in every space exploration journey (flight). Thus, the energy will be space transportation tool one important factor. If the space transportation tool has enough supply, which won't stay in space and can not fly in space suddenly. Thus, the every time of the human space flight will be taken more time and effort then would be reasonable to expect prior to return to flight. Thus, human space exploration organization needs have higher reliability organization structure to manage every space flight, e.g. one is separating technical authority from the function of managing schedules and cost. Another is an independent safety and mission assurance organization.

It is the capability for effective systems integration perhaps even more challenging than these organizational changes are the cultural changes requires. Thus, the cultural to safe and effective space rocket operations are real and substantial. If the space exploration organization has good culture to let every staffs can communicate easily. I believe the every time space exploration accident will be reduced. Examples include: the tendency to keep knowledge of problems contained within a center or program, technical decisions, without in -depth, peer-reviewed technical analysis, and an unofficial hierarchy or system created by placing excessive power in one office. Such factors interfere with open communication, the shared of lesson learned, cause duplication and expenditure of resources and create a burden for managers to reduce undesirable characteristics threaten safety.

Thus, any space exploration trip, rocket equipment safety and check are very important factor to prepare for every time space flight. The reason is that space flight must guarantee any space people who can come back Earth, if the rocket equipment are poor and lack maintenance. The, the space people whose life is dangerous. Due any space exploration organization mission require human presence in space. For example, president John Kennedy's 1961 charge to send Americans to the moon and return then safely to Earth. Thus, the space exploration organization has attempted to carry out a similar high priority mission that would justify the expenditure of resources on a scale equivalent to those allocated for project Apollo. Also, the space exploration organization has had to participate in the give and take of the normal political process in order to obtain the resources needed to carry out its programs.

Another main successful factor in the final stage, the space exploration organization needs have a clearly defined long term space mission to commit over the past decade to improve future space exploration flight safety by developing a second generation space transportation system. So, for long term, the space exploration organization should need to plan for future space transportation capabilities without making them dependent on technological breakthroughs.

For example, mission for a post Apollo effort that involved full development of low-Earth orbit, permanent outposts on the moon, and initial journeys to Mars planet. Since that rejection, these objective, have reappeared as central elements in many proposals, setting a long term vision for any space exploration flight programs in the future.

Thus, space organization future space exploration mission for 21 St century is to lead the exploration and development of the space frontier, advance science, technology and enterprise and building institutions and systems that make accessible vast new resources and support human settlements beyond Earth orbit from the highland of the Moon to the plains of Mars. Thus, the space exploration organization limit is to conduct the research required to plan missions to Mars and/or other distant destinations. This is the most safe space flight distance limit by the space rocket equipment, machine installation , quality and effort to guarantee space people life safety when who catch the space rocket life safety when who catch the rocket to leave Earth to arrive any space destination in any space flight. However, human travel to destinations beyond Earth orbit has not been adopted because it is too far space flight to cause accident risk. Hence, space exploration organization future invention of long term need is that the role of new space transportation capabilities in enabling whatever space goals need to choose to pursue for human present in Earth orbit vision.

In conclusion, space exploration organization needs to in-depth examination space shuttle safe issue, how to reach an inescapable design of the space shuttle, because that the design was based in many aspects on how absolute technologies and because the space shutter is now an aging system , but still developmental in character, it is in the space organization is interest to replace the shuttle as soon as possible as the primary aim for transporting humans to and from Earth orbit.

CHAPTER EIGHT

SPACE EXPLORATION ORGANIZATION MISSION AND STRATEGY

Space exploration organization communication strategy
I recommend any space exploration organization needs to the message concerns how the role of humans are actual physical presence in space exploration missions succeed. Because the positive message will give good idea of space exploration and then design and build means to carry out right space exploration direction to let humans to know whether any space exploration missions' goals, objectives and what humans benefits (welfares) who can earn.

The message includes such as these primary role of humans, therefore, is to provide the inspiration and create the vision which produces the motivation in those who then go on to make it a reality, e.g. the space exploration mission is to bring their human intellectual capability to bear in designing the technical systems required for space transportation and devising the scientific experiments associated with space exploration from its beginnings.

Thus, any space exploration organization needs to let humans to know whether what benefits humans will earn after it carries out any space exploration experiments possibly. I believe that the exploration of the Earth's great expanse (the sea, the undersea world, air and land) is the ultimate role played by humans in body and in mind, and apply their intelligence, emotions and most importantly of all, their superior cognitive performance. So, this is the role now played by astronauts, explorers in the true sense of the world.

Why does space exploration organization need to be the role of communicator? The reason is because there is the role that space organization's need to play as communicators, journalists or other communication professional. It is they who provide the link between those involved in the project and taxpayer, who are entitled to be informed about the fascinating news on space.

Moreover, space exploration organization staffs need to give message to let humans to know why these playing roles are entirely human specific and can not be fulfilled by machines. For example, roles prior to human intervention, such as accompanying humans and performing tasks, which are repetitive and unpleasant out satellites too high a risk. By sending out satellites to explore our solar system humans have already begun to explore universe into reality Robots. On the other hand, may be things, but they are not visionaries and nor are they inventors or explorers. Any achievement they accomplish are in fact space organization staffs who designed and programmed them. Also, humans remain the best available cognitive machine in any environment that may be subject to significant variations relative to the model initially made of it. Thus, space exploration organization needs to explain, such as why in the general context of space exploration, even of most missions are robotic, remains technology challenges, it presents push engineers to the very limits of what can be achieved.

In the future, humans will earn these benefits or from any space explorations new invention possibly, such as fuel cells, the microcomputer, high performance materials, medical advances, new management techniques for major projects, quality and reliability control in industry etc.

The most important space exploration organization needs to positive message to let these groups of people to human what which is doing in our societies. Then, which will cause different actors to become involved from thinkers, visionaries and inspirational figures in the form of writers and film makers to scientists, engineers, philosophers, politicians, economists, physicians, journalists, authors, space travelers (astronauts), but also adults and children space story book readers alike. Thus, space exploration organization is truly multi disciplinary enterprise. Moreover, in the present day, normal escapes being concerned by space, as much due to its contribution to daily life and the knowledge it beings of the Solar system and the universe. It seems space exploration organization will influence human past history will be changed to develop. Whether it brings positive or negative change. The space organization must have responsibility to keep its any space exploration missions leader position in our Earth. It implies it is also one social responsible organization for future global human benefit (welfare).

Also space exploration organization needs to let humans know what it's future aims (intentions) are to let humans know whether why it plan to implement. Such as it needs to choose destination has typically been the Moon, it had increasingly come to focus its attention on Mars and even further afraid. Moreover, it also needs to know humans to know the modes of future space transportation which described have tended to be those of the period concerned: ships, horses, birds, balloons, canons, rockets and even others of a more esoteric nature, even solar sail or nuclear soil further space transportation technology development. In addition, space exploration organization can need to describe where are further orbital space stations in space different locations and explained the various applications of satellites and spacecrafts to let human to know clearly.

Even, space exploration organization also need to let humans to know what are their technical challenges, it will encounter in any space exploration stages to let humans to know. Although, the complexity and changer involved in spaceflight is such for a long time to come there will be a need for experts, whose focus by necessity. So, the general public will know or recognize why it's technical challenges will cause and how it will attempt to solve these technical challenges. It aims to let humans to ensure more than 40 years of spaceflight, the adventive of space, which for technical reasons is inevitably reserved to a " happy few", remains very much the preserve of specialists, cooperation to research how to solve any technical challenges to achieve success in any space exploration mission consequently.

● Space exploration organization team leaders and their

teams

The first team members are program chiefs and mission message are request to the be backroom generals with a great many human qualities. They must having to achieve great technical exploits and manage their teams with care when at the same time ensuring they deliver in timing and one budget. Even the very best robot-machines and computers available are of no help to them in coming up with the initial idea and architecture for their systems. Indeed, in that initial stages, some program chiefs, even insist on their management team using only paper and pencil writing. Once the concept has been defined, they then need computers to speed up and develop the project. When these leader figures are fortunate enough to see their program in orbit and crowned with success, their experience and methods can be of use, to equally computer technical sectors. They can also be passed on to following generations, thus safeguarding, for reasons of economics and security, the know how acquired by their teams. Another team members are scientists and those responsible for the technical side of program are not generally skilled communicators by nature, those with communication to public , such " communicators" could be awarded special prizes. Communication on the space sector can't be left to " communication specialists". Otherwise, there is a risk, it will be perceived to be doomed to failure.

Space exploration organization education is such as strategy space exploration organization communicator, are there to inform, the teaching profession for its part, must perform a vital education role, helping people understand the universe in which they live. Space exploration represents a unique opportunity to explain the situation of our planet within the solar system, asking questions such as: How does the sun function? What are the origins of the Moon? Why does Venus have such a pronounced greenhouse effect? Is there or has there ever been life on Mars? Do asteroids pose a serious threat? There are all questions which today, our schools don't even attempt to answer. Thus, space exploration organization can be one educator role, instead of space explorer role.

Thus, space exploration organization has mission to assist universities to promote space exploration education knowledges. It brings this question: What other technological and scientific program is better equipped to meet these objective than space exploration , with its crewed emissions component. So crucial to the promotion of a European industry, so visible to the general public and so efficient in inducing younger generations to take up scientific and technical careers? Thus, the space education courses can include space exploration industrial applications, a new area of investigation to scientific fields, fundamental physics, cellular and vegetal biomedical research and human and animal physiological research etc. subjects. For example, teaching how to go to Mars or other planets and manage to live these will require a knowledge of how to energy in innovative ways for the purposes of managing electricity generation requirement will be to learn how to manage scare resources in an efficient way (air, water and waste recycling). So, teaching of progress will have to be made in advanced robotics in particular in the area of effective and human robot interaction.

In conclusion, all these space exploration science education knowledge will be important to be taught to let younger to pursue space resource exploration dream for human future live

SPACE EXPLORATION ORGANIZATION'S HUMAN SPACE LIFE SCIENCE FACTOR

What is human space life science strategy?

One space exploration organization needs have good human resource strategy to implement every space exploration mission. Critical to this expansion of human presence in space science will enable mission success by focusing on risk reduction and optimizing astronaut health an productivity through space organization's human-centered science, operations and engineering core capabilities.

Thus, the space life science strategy's strategical goals, and objectives were developed on the basis of a situational analysis conducted by key members of the space life science civil service and contractor

community, and are consistent with agency goals and scenarios for the future.

This strategy mission is to optimize human health and productivity for space exploration and its vision is to become the recognized world leader in human health, performance and productivity for space exploration . It's strategic goal are aimed at driving innovations in health and human system integration, adapting its portfolio and strategies to the changing environment and creating enthusiasm for space exploration through education. Also, the space life sciences human strategy aims to achieve every space exploration research more success, more efficient, focuses on client (human) needs and facilities communication of risk to public and the value of space life sciences to its stakeholders (governments, universities, societies).

How can human space life science strategy implement?

The space exploration organization needs to be dependent upon healthy, productive astronauts to achieve mission success. Thus, space people health are very important factor to influence their every time space flight in success. If the space people have unhealthy bodies , which will influence whose work performance and every time space exploration mission can't finish easily. Thus, the human space life science strategy needs to ensure every space person has health body to work efficiently and reduce whose death or accident risk when they are working in space environment, due to space environment is one strange bad color environment and it is very difference to our Earth environment to unsafe to work by these factors:

such as, it's temperature is low, cold and no air or oxygen to be supplied to let human to breathe and it has unknown diseases in space. Thus, they will face any life danger when are working in space environment. If space organization lacks one human space life science strategy to help them to fight any unknown attack from space environment. The, they are very dangerous to attempt to catch space rockets to leave our Earth to do any space exploration activities.

However, the space life science strategy can divide these three timeframes consistent with

- Near –term (1-5 years)
- Mid-term (6-10 years)
- Long-term (11-20 years)

The space life science strategy mission is that optimize human health and productivity for space exploration . Thus, all space life sciences human health and countermeasures research, medical operations, habitability and environmental factors activities, and directorate support functions are ultimately aimed at achieving this mission. Their activities enable mission success, optimizing human health and productivity in space before, during and after the actual space flight experience of their flight crews, and include support for ground-based functions.

The space life science strategy vision is to become the recognized world leader in human health, performance and productivity for space exploration. Thus, to achieve the vision for space exploration , they must drive human health, performance and productivity innovations, adapting their strategy to the changing environment. To do this, the space exploration organization needs have a future scenario for space life science strategy such as below:

● Future core capabilities will include the expertise to address space medicine, the physiological and behavioral effects of space flight, space environment definition and space human factors.

● Research plans are on the basis of a standard –based risk mitigation approach to ensure goals are achieved.

● Civil servants will balance delivery of health and performance services and focused research and technology development with smart buyer and management expertise to integrate space life sciences efforts.

● Strategy relationships will be utilized to achieve the full complement of space life sciences core

capabilities necessary to achieve vision and enable mission success.

● Space life science strategy will transition from being a managing partner to a contributing partner, arranging the resources and innovations of other organizations to meet specific exploration needs, e.g. universities, government or business biomedicine organizations.

● Operations will effectively transition the space people skills and facilities from shuttle and assess and engage in additional government and commercial space flight operations opportunities where appropriate.

● An expanded client base that may include additional international and academic partners , as well as commercial alliances.

● Situation analysis

A situation analysis was conducted to determine its mission and to identify the factors most likely to influence its strategy development and affect achievement of its goals and objectives . It will trend to concern life sciences and space flight of internal and external environments. It needs to image these assumptions to decide its situation analysis as below:

Thus, the first assumption is that it needs to assume that human will continue to be an important component of the vision for space exploration, and as a result there will be an ongoing need for space life sciences core capabilities, including human-centered science, operations and engineering to mitigate the health and performance risk of human space flight.

Another assumption is in the longer term, there will be a greater focus on crew autonomy and increased human-robotics interaction as mission durations increase and are extended to travel to and on planets, and as a result, these is a continued need for research and development activity focused need for research and development activity focused on exploration risk reduction.

The next assumption is the pace of biomedical change will continue to be more rapid in external versus internal environments. Thus, solutions are more kinds of likely to be developed external to fight any different new unknown new diseases to attack to influence space people health to be poor , even cause death in possible.

● What are space life science strategy goals?

On health innovation hands, the space exploration organization will drive advances in medical and environmental health for space flight in order to meet established space life standard and mission needs. Thus , innovation on medicine and biomedical / environment technology and processes will be developed, implement and incorporated into mission achievement.

On education hand, it needs to train in multidisciplinary life sciences, experts in exploration life science and that this is a continuous infusion of space ,life science into the public , government , academic and commercial sectors. Thus, the space life science education aim includes to teach the human system risk management, strategic relationship of any space missions, future space business model and space communication strategies.

The goal-specific strategies and measurable objectives can be developed for years 1 to 5 years It's objectives can include: optimize internal core capabilities throughout the planning cycle to enable the vision for space exploration with budgetary constraints, establish strategic relationship to achieve the full complement of life sciences capabilities necessary to be best in class , establish a center to integrate human health and performance efforts and expertise for space exploration worldwide, implement an internal and external communication plan to increase the life sciences value to encourage space human life education development for long term in commercial space flight sector.

● Health innovation goal

Thus, one space exploration organization whose health innovation strategy is the main factor to influence its any overall space exploration missions inn success. Thus, it must need to spend more money and time and resource to ensure its health innovation implement can be succeed to reduce further every time space people's mission of physical illness or death or accident which are caused by space diseases . Thus, it will drive advances in medical and environmental health for space flight in order to meet establish space flight health standards and mission needs. Also, it needs to attempt to do any biomedical experiments to avoid space people who can contact to cause illness from any undiscovered space diseases.

Hence, the invention of space medicine, biomedical / space environmental technology and processes will be developed, implemented often every day/ IT needs to seek or gather every time practical space environment biomedical existing data and knowledge as a base for launching health technologies and to revise every time space biomedical experiment failure to find failure reasons to achieve the most absolute discovered any space unknown diseases biomedical experiment results. Thus, the improved methods and practice or recording data must concern to goals for human space exploration, attempting towards data gathering top continuing to achieve the best levels of evidence for answering operational and clinical questions regarding human health, safety and performance, during space flight and exploration and an evidence-based risk management approach to prioritize tasks.

The space biomedical experiments data gathering can consider human factors engineering, habitability design and human-robotics interaction will be recorded to analyze experiment result every time. These results will be developed, implemented and incorporated into mission architecture solutions to address the human as an element of the overall space system.

● Prediction on future trends in human space flight and future space human life science strategy relationship.

In the future, the relationship between future trends in human space flight and future space human life science will be more close. These reasons are that the trends in terrestrial life sciences will save as change drivers for space life sciences, include advanced in nano health, genetics, biocybernetics, self-constructing materials, human computer interfaces, medical and pharmaco-therapeutics, multi-scale physiological modelling and other biomedical technologies.

In conclusion, due to space exploration organization's objective is low tolerance for a risk and emphasis on risk quantification and reduction activities. Thus, the space human life science

strategy will be one important factors to cause any one space exploration organization's any missions in success.

● Why does Japan space organization consider space human life science?

Japan has acquired and advanced various space technologies. Through, these technologies level to allow to play a core role in the international human space activities . However, it's space exploration success is due to it concerns to achieve its space human life science strategy for its main point.

What social benefit from its utilization of the space environment to Japan. Because it concerns how to protect space human life during who are working in space. Thus, it can bring more social benefits to develop its space exploration industry for long term as below:

● Because it's space people can have health bodied, so who can attempt to any space science exploration experiments in space

environment as well as space human life science can raise Japan space people confidence to attempt to do every time space exploration activities in space environment. Consequently, they have confidence to catch rockets to go to space to gather various resource to do any space exploration to get research results more easily, which were achieved through utilization , such as micro gravity environment, that could not be produced on the ground, these outcomes include: protein crystal growth, that may lead to the development of new drugs, materials creation for next-generation semi-conductors, and establishment of the technology for cubesats deployment, etc.

● Due to Japan space exploration organization concerns space people health issue. Thus, it has manned space flight capability can conduct youth development activities , with their own astronauts and such astronaut-led activities have aroused the younger generation's interest in outer space, taught them the importance of making efforts to making of one health space scientists confidence to pursue this space exploration industry.

Hence, when all Japan space scientists who own health bodies, then who can be one expansion of humankind's space of activities in this area create knowledge of planetary science and the quest of health space life and also contributes to the increase and accumulation of intellectual assets of all human beings.

The most reason of Japan's belief of space human life science strategy is very important , because it needs to prove human can live in space environment. Thus, if Japan's space scientists can have health bodies to do any space exploration experiments, then who is still health to go back

Earth. Then , it proves the life support technologies , the space environment and health management and the maximum energy conservation. This leads to the enhancement of corporate brands and international appeal of technical capabilities , and is directly linked to resulting problems Japan faces , such as its aging population and lack of natural resources.

In conclusion, space human life science will influence Japan space exploration industry more success. Otherwise, if it chooses not to implement this space human life strategy. It won't have enough health space scientists to attempt to catch rockets to go to space to do any space exploration experiments more success in long term, e.g. seeking Earth another planets to provide Japan people to live, raising Japan young space scientists confidence to attempt to go to space to do any experiments because the Japan space exploration organization can provide new bio medical invention to supply when they are catching in the space rockets. If they feel that they are comfortable, they can eat or drink the new bio medical invention to avoid the space disease attack to cause their death or physical illness threat.

In conclusion, space human life science is very important factor to influence future every time human space exploration mission successfully.